50 Irresistible Ramen Recipes

By: Kelly Johnson

Table of Contents

- Shoyu Ramen
- Miso Ramen
- Tonkotsu Ramen
- Spicy Miso Ramen
- Shio Ramen
- Chicken Ramen
- Beef Ramen
- Seafood Ramen
- Vegetarian Ramen
- Kimchi Ramen
- Coconut Curry Ramen
- Teriyaki Chicken Ramen
- Sesame Garlic Ramen
- Creamy Garlic Ramen
- Tonkotsu Shoyu Ramen
- Ramen Noodle Salad
- Egg Drop Ramen
- Spicy Peanut Ramen
- Chili Oil Ramen
- Bacon Ramen
- Ramen Carbonara
- Sriracha Ramen
- Miso Butter Ramen
- Thai Coconut Ramen
- Gyoza Ramen
- Teriyaki Salmon Ramen
- Grilled Vegetable Ramen
- Ramen with Soft-Boiled Eggs
- Shrimp Tempura Ramen
- Curry Udon Ramen
- Roasted Pork Ramen
- Tofu Ramen
- Spicy Kimchi Tofu Ramen
- Lobster Ramen
- Ramen with Dashi Broth
- Lemon Chicken Ramen

- Duck Ramen
- Creamy Spinach Ramen
- Sweet Potato Ramen
- Cilantro Lime Ramen
- Beef Brisket Ramen
- Ramen with Braised Egg
- Sichuan Spicy Ramen
- Buffalo Chicken Ramen
- Ramen with Pickled Vegetables
- Black Garlic Ramen
- Garlic Butter Ramen
- Smoked Salmon Ramen
- Ramen with Roasted Corn
- Cilantro Coconut Ramen

Shoyu Ramen

Ingredients

- 4 cups chicken broth
- 2 cups water
- 1/4 cup soy sauce
- 2 tbsp mirin
- 1 tbsp sesame oil
- 2 packs ramen noodles
- 2 green onions, sliced
- 2 soft-boiled eggs
- Nori sheets, for garnish
- Sliced cooked pork or chicken (optional)

Instructions

1. **Prepare Broth:** In a large pot, combine chicken broth, water, soy sauce, mirin, and sesame oil. Bring to a simmer over medium heat.
2. **Cook Noodles:** Cook ramen noodles according to package instructions. Drain and set aside.
3. **Assemble Bowls:** Divide noodles among serving bowls. Ladle hot broth over the noodles.
4. **Garnish:** Top with sliced green onions, soft-boiled eggs, nori, and sliced meat if desired. Serve hot.

Miso Ramen

Ingredients

- 4 cups chicken broth
- 2 tbsp miso paste
- 1 tbsp soy sauce
- 2 packs ramen noodles
- 1 cup bean sprouts
- 2 green onions, sliced
- 2 soft-boiled eggs
- Chashu pork, for garnish (optional)

Instructions

1. **Prepare Broth:** In a pot, heat chicken broth over medium heat. Stir in miso paste and soy sauce until fully dissolved.
2. **Cook Noodles:** Cook ramen noodles as per package instructions. Drain and set aside.
3. **Assemble Bowls:** Divide cooked noodles among bowls. Pour hot miso broth over noodles.
4. **Garnish:** Top with bean sprouts, green onions, soft-boiled eggs, and chashu pork if using. Serve immediately.

Tonkotsu Ramen

Ingredients

- 4 cups pork bone broth
- 2 packs ramen noodles
- 1/4 cup soy sauce
- 2 tbsp mirin
- 1 cup sliced mushrooms
- 2 green onions, sliced
- 2 soft-boiled eggs
- Chashu pork, for garnish

Instructions

1. **Prepare Broth:** In a pot, heat pork bone broth over medium heat. Add soy sauce and mirin.
2. **Cook Noodles:** Cook ramen noodles according to package directions. Drain and set aside.
3. **Assemble Bowls:** Divide noodles among bowls. Pour hot tonkotsu broth over noodles.
4. **Garnish:** Top with mushrooms, green onions, soft-boiled eggs, and chashu pork. Serve hot.

Spicy Miso Ramen

Ingredients

- 4 cups chicken broth
- 2 tbsp miso paste
- 1 tbsp chili paste (or to taste)
- 2 packs ramen noodles
- 1 cup spinach
- 2 green onions, sliced
- 2 soft-boiled eggs
- Sriracha, for garnish (optional)

Instructions

1. **Prepare Broth:** In a pot, heat chicken broth over medium heat. Whisk in miso paste and chili paste until fully combined.
2. **Cook Noodles:** Prepare ramen noodles according to package instructions. Drain and set aside.
3. **Assemble Bowls:** Place noodles in bowls and ladle hot spicy miso broth over them.
4. **Garnish:** Top with spinach, green onions, soft-boiled eggs, and a drizzle of Sriracha if desired.

Shio Ramen

Ingredients

- 4 cups chicken broth
- 1/4 cup salt (adjust to taste)
- 2 packs ramen noodles
- 1 cup sliced bamboo shoots
- 2 green onions, sliced
- 2 soft-boiled eggs
- Chashu pork or chicken, for garnish

Instructions

1. **Prepare Broth:** In a pot, combine chicken broth and salt. Bring to a simmer over medium heat.
2. **Cook Noodles:** Cook ramen noodles as per package instructions. Drain and set aside.
3. **Assemble Bowls:** Divide noodles into serving bowls. Pour hot shio broth over the noodles.
4. **Garnish:** Top with bamboo shoots, green onions, soft-boiled eggs, and chashu pork or chicken. Serve immediately.

Chicken Ramen

Ingredients

- 4 cups chicken broth
- 2 packs ramen noodles
- 1 cup cooked chicken, shredded
- 1/4 cup soy sauce
- 2 green onions, sliced
- 2 soft-boiled eggs
- Spinach or bok choy, for garnish

Instructions

1. **Prepare Broth:** In a pot, heat chicken broth over medium heat. Stir in soy sauce.
2. **Cook Noodles:** Cook ramen noodles according to package directions. Drain and set aside.
3. **Assemble Bowls:** Divide noodles among bowls, add shredded chicken, and pour hot broth over.
4. **Garnish:** Top with green onions, soft-boiled eggs, and spinach or bok choy. Serve hot.

Beef Ramen

Ingredients

- 4 cups beef broth
- 2 packs ramen noodles
- 1 cup cooked beef, sliced thin
- 1/4 cup soy sauce
- 1 cup sliced mushrooms
- 2 green onions, sliced
- 2 soft-boiled eggs

Instructions

1. **Prepare Broth:** In a pot, heat beef broth over medium heat. Stir in soy sauce.
2. **Cook Noodles:** Cook ramen noodles according to package directions. Drain and set aside.
3. **Assemble Bowls:** Place noodles in bowls, add sliced beef, and pour hot broth over.
4. **Garnish:** Top with mushrooms, green onions, and soft-boiled eggs. Serve hot.

Seafood Ramen

Ingredients

- 4 cups seafood broth
- 2 packs ramen noodles
- 1 cup mixed seafood (shrimp, scallops, etc.)
- 1/4 cup soy sauce
- 1 cup bok choy
- 2 green onions, sliced
- 2 soft-boiled eggs

Instructions

1. **Prepare Broth:** In a pot, heat seafood broth over medium heat. Stir in soy sauce.
2. **Cook Noodles:** Cook ramen noodles as per package instructions. Drain and set aside.
3. **Assemble Bowls:** Place noodles in bowls, add mixed seafood, and pour hot broth over.
4. **Garnish:** Top with bok choy, green onions, and soft-boiled eggs. Serve immediately.

Vegetarian Ramen

Ingredients

- 4 cups vegetable broth
- 2 packs ramen noodles
- 1 cup sliced mushrooms
- 1 cup spinach
- 1/4 cup soy sauce
- 2 green onions, sliced
- 1 cup bean sprouts
- Soft-boiled egg, for garnish (optional)

Instructions

1. **Prepare Broth:** In a pot, heat vegetable broth over medium heat. Add soy sauce and mushrooms, cooking until mushrooms are tender.
2. **Cook Noodles:** Cook ramen noodles according to package instructions. Drain and set aside.
3. **Assemble Bowls:** Divide noodles among serving bowls and ladle hot broth over them.
4. **Garnish:** Top with spinach, green onions, bean sprouts, and a soft-boiled egg if desired. Serve hot.

Kimchi Ramen

Ingredients

- 4 cups chicken or vegetable broth
- 2 packs ramen noodles
- 1 cup kimchi
- 1/4 cup soy sauce
- 2 green onions, sliced
- 2 soft-boiled eggs
- Sesame seeds, for garnish

Instructions

1. **Prepare Broth:** In a pot, heat broth over medium heat. Stir in kimchi and soy sauce, simmering for about 5 minutes.
2. **Cook Noodles:** Cook ramen noodles according to package instructions. Drain and set aside.
3. **Assemble Bowls:** Place noodles in bowls and pour the hot kimchi broth over them.
4. **Garnish:** Top with green onions, soft-boiled eggs, and sesame seeds. Serve hot.

Coconut Curry Ramen

Ingredients

- 4 cups vegetable broth
- 1 can (14 oz) coconut milk
- 2 tbsp red curry paste
- 2 packs ramen noodles
- 1 cup sliced bell peppers
- 1 cup spinach
- Lime wedges, for serving

Instructions

1. **Prepare Broth:** In a pot, combine vegetable broth, coconut milk, and red curry paste. Heat over medium heat until simmering.
2. **Cook Noodles:** Cook ramen noodles according to package instructions. Drain and set aside.
3. **Add Vegetables:** Stir in bell peppers and spinach into the broth, cooking until just tender.
4. **Assemble Bowls:** Divide noodles among bowls and ladle hot coconut curry broth over them. Serve with lime wedges.

Teriyaki Chicken Ramen

Ingredients

- 4 cups chicken broth
- 2 packs ramen noodles
- 1 cup cooked chicken, shredded
- 1/4 cup teriyaki sauce
- 1 cup broccoli florets
- 2 green onions, sliced

Instructions

1. **Prepare Broth:** In a pot, heat chicken broth over medium heat. Stir in teriyaki sauce.
2. **Cook Noodles:** Cook ramen noodles according to package instructions. Drain and set aside.
3. **Add Chicken and Broccoli:** Add shredded chicken and broccoli to the broth, simmering until broccoli is tender.
4. **Assemble Bowls:** Divide noodles among serving bowls and pour the hot teriyaki broth over them. Garnish with green onions.

Sesame Garlic Ramen

Ingredients

- 4 cups chicken or vegetable broth
- 2 packs ramen noodles
- 3 cloves garlic, minced
- 2 tbsp sesame oil
- 1/4 cup soy sauce
- 2 green onions, sliced
- Sesame seeds, for garnish

Instructions

1. **Prepare Broth:** In a pot, heat chicken or vegetable broth over medium heat. Add minced garlic, soy sauce, and sesame oil.
2. **Cook Noodles:** Cook ramen noodles according to package instructions. Drain and set aside.
3. **Assemble Bowls:** Divide noodles among serving bowls and ladle hot broth over them.
4. **Garnish:** Top with green onions and sprinkle with sesame seeds. Serve hot.

Creamy Garlic Ramen

Ingredients

- 4 cups chicken broth
- 2 packs ramen noodles
- 3 cloves garlic, minced
- 1 cup heavy cream
- 1/4 cup grated Parmesan cheese
- 2 green onions, sliced

Instructions

1. **Prepare Broth:** In a pot, heat chicken broth over medium heat. Add minced garlic and simmer for 5 minutes.
2. **Add Cream:** Stir in heavy cream and Parmesan cheese, cooking until smooth.
3. **Cook Noodles:** Cook ramen noodles according to package instructions. Drain and set aside.
4. **Assemble Bowls:** Divide noodles among bowls and ladle the creamy garlic broth over them. Garnish with green onions.

Tonkotsu Shoyu Ramen

Ingredients

- 4 cups pork bone broth
- 2 packs ramen noodles
- 1/4 cup soy sauce
- 1 tbsp mirin
- 1 cup sliced mushrooms
- 2 green onions, sliced
- Chashu pork, for garnish

Instructions

1. **Prepare Broth:** In a pot, heat pork bone broth over medium heat. Add soy sauce and mirin.
2. **Cook Noodles:** Cook ramen noodles according to package instructions. Drain and set aside.
3. **Assemble Bowls:** Divide noodles among bowls and pour hot tonkotsu broth over them.
4. **Garnish:** Top with mushrooms, green onions, and chashu pork. Serve hot.

Ramen Noodle Salad

Ingredients

- 2 packs ramen noodles
- 2 cups mixed vegetables (carrots, bell peppers, cabbage)
- 1/4 cup soy sauce
- 2 tbsp sesame oil
- 2 tbsp rice vinegar
- 2 green onions, sliced
- Sesame seeds, for garnish

Instructions

1. **Cook Noodles:** Cook ramen noodles according to package instructions. Drain and rinse under cold water.
2. **Prepare Dressing:** In a bowl, whisk together soy sauce, sesame oil, and rice vinegar.
3. **Combine Salad:** In a large bowl, combine noodles, mixed vegetables, and dressing. Toss to combine.
4. **Garnish:** Serve topped with green onions and sesame seeds. Enjoy cold or at room temperature.

Egg Drop Ramen

Ingredients

- 4 cups chicken broth
- 2 packs ramen noodles
- 2 eggs
- 1 cup spinach
- 1/4 cup soy sauce
- 2 green onions, sliced
- Sesame oil, for garnish

Instructions

1. **Prepare Broth:** In a pot, heat chicken broth over medium heat.
2. **Cook Noodles:** Add ramen noodles and cook according to package instructions.
3. **Add Spinach:** Stir in spinach until wilted.
4. **Add Eggs:** Beat eggs in a bowl, then slowly drizzle into the broth while stirring gently to create egg ribbons.
5. **Season and Serve:** Stir in soy sauce, and serve hot, garnished with green onions and a drizzle of sesame oil.

Spicy Peanut Ramen

Ingredients

- 4 cups chicken or vegetable broth
- 2 packs ramen noodles
- 1/2 cup creamy peanut butter
- 2 tbsp soy sauce
- 1 tbsp sriracha (or more to taste)
- 1 cup shredded carrots
- 2 green onions, sliced

Instructions

1. **Prepare Broth:** In a pot, heat chicken or vegetable broth over medium heat. Stir in peanut butter, soy sauce, and sriracha until smooth.
2. **Cook Noodles:** Add ramen noodles and cook according to package instructions.
3. **Add Carrots:** Stir in shredded carrots until heated through.
4. **Serve:** Divide among bowls and garnish with green onions. Enjoy hot!

Chili Oil Ramen

Ingredients

- 4 cups chicken broth
- 2 packs ramen noodles
- 1/4 cup chili oil
- 2 cloves garlic, minced
- 1 tbsp soy sauce
- 2 green onions, sliced
- Soft-boiled egg, for garnish (optional)

Instructions

1. **Prepare Broth:** In a pot, heat chicken broth over medium heat. Add minced garlic and cook until fragrant.
2. **Cook Noodles:** Add ramen noodles and cook according to package instructions.
3. **Add Chili Oil:** Stir in chili oil and soy sauce, mixing well.
4. **Serve:** Divide among bowls, top with green onions and a soft-boiled egg if desired. Enjoy hot!

Bacon Ramen

Ingredients

- 4 cups chicken broth
- 2 packs ramen noodles
- 4 strips of bacon, chopped
- 2 green onions, sliced
- 1/4 cup soy sauce
- Soft-boiled egg, for garnish

Instructions

1. **Cook Bacon:** In a pot, cook chopped bacon over medium heat until crispy. Remove and set aside, leaving the fat in the pot.
2. **Prepare Broth:** Add chicken broth to the pot and bring to a simmer.
3. **Cook Noodles:** Add ramen noodles and cook according to package instructions.
4. **Serve:** Divide noodles among bowls, pour broth over, and top with bacon, green onions, and a soft-boiled egg. Enjoy hot!

Ramen Carbonara

Ingredients

- 4 cups chicken broth
- 2 packs ramen noodles
- 4 slices of pancetta or bacon, diced
- 2 eggs
- 1/2 cup grated Parmesan cheese
- Black pepper, to taste
- Fresh parsley, for garnish

Instructions

1. **Cook Pancetta:** In a pot, cook pancetta or bacon over medium heat until crispy. Remove and set aside.
2. **Prepare Broth:** Add chicken broth to the pot and bring to a simmer.
3. **Cook Noodles:** Add ramen noodles and cook according to package instructions.
4. **Mix Eggs and Cheese:** In a bowl, whisk together eggs, Parmesan cheese, and black pepper.
5. **Combine:** Drain noodles, then quickly mix with the egg mixture, stirring vigorously to create a creamy sauce.
6. **Serve:** Top with pancetta and garnish with parsley. Enjoy hot!

Sriracha Ramen

Ingredients

- 4 cups chicken broth
- 2 packs ramen noodles
- 2 tbsp sriracha (or more to taste)
- 1 cup sliced bok choy
- 2 green onions, sliced
- Soft-boiled egg, for garnish (optional)

Instructions

1. **Prepare Broth:** In a pot, heat chicken broth over medium heat. Stir in sriracha to combine.
2. **Cook Noodles:** Add ramen noodles and cook according to package instructions.
3. **Add Bok Choy:** Stir in bok choy and cook until tender.
4. **Serve:** Divide among bowls and top with green onions and a soft-boiled egg if desired. Enjoy hot!

Miso Butter Ramen

Ingredients

- 4 cups chicken broth
- 2 packs ramen noodles
- 2 tbsp miso paste
- 2 tbsp butter
- 1 cup mushrooms, sliced
- 2 green onions, sliced

Instructions

1. **Prepare Broth:** In a pot, heat chicken broth over medium heat. Whisk in miso paste and butter until smooth.
2. **Cook Noodles:** Add ramen noodles and cook according to package instructions.
3. **Add Mushrooms:** Stir in sliced mushrooms and cook until tender.
4. **Serve:** Divide among bowls and garnish with green onions. Enjoy hot!

Thai Coconut Ramen

Ingredients

- 4 cups vegetable broth
- 1 can (14 oz) coconut milk
- 2 packs ramen noodles
- 1 tbsp red curry paste
- 1 cup sliced bell peppers
- 2 green onions, sliced

Instructions

1. **Prepare Broth:** In a pot, combine vegetable broth, coconut milk, and red curry paste. Heat over medium heat until simmering.
2. **Cook Noodles:** Add ramen noodles and cook according to package instructions.
3. **Add Bell Peppers:** Stir in sliced bell peppers and cook until tender.
4. **Serve:** Divide among bowls and garnish with green onions. Enjoy hot!

Gyoza Ramen

Ingredients

- 4 cups chicken broth
- 2 packs ramen noodles
- 8 gyoza (dumplings), cooked
- 1 cup bok choy, chopped
- 2 green onions, sliced
- Soy sauce, to taste
- Sesame oil, for garnish

Instructions

1. **Prepare Broth:** In a pot, heat chicken broth over medium heat.
2. **Cook Noodles:** Add ramen noodles and cook according to package instructions.
3. **Add Bok Choy:** Stir in bok choy and cook until wilted.
4. **Serve:** Divide noodles among bowls, add gyoza, and season with soy sauce. Drizzle with sesame oil before serving.

Teriyaki Salmon Ramen

Ingredients

- 4 cups chicken or vegetable broth
- 2 packs ramen noodles
- 2 salmon fillets
- 1/4 cup teriyaki sauce
- 1 cup spinach
- Sesame seeds, for garnish
- Green onions, sliced

Instructions

1. **Cook Salmon:** In a skillet, cook salmon fillets over medium heat, brushing with teriyaki sauce, until cooked through.
2. **Prepare Broth:** In a pot, heat chicken or vegetable broth over medium heat.
3. **Cook Noodles:** Add ramen noodles and cook according to package instructions.
4. **Add Spinach:** Stir in spinach until wilted.
5. **Serve:** Divide noodles among bowls, top with salmon, and garnish with sesame seeds and green onions.

Grilled Vegetable Ramen

Ingredients

- 4 cups vegetable broth
- 2 packs ramen noodles
- 1 cup mixed vegetables (bell peppers, zucchini, mushrooms), grilled
- 2 tbsp soy sauce
- 2 green onions, sliced
- Chili flakes, for garnish

Instructions

1. **Prepare Broth:** In a pot, heat vegetable broth over medium heat.
2. **Cook Noodles:** Add ramen noodles and cook according to package instructions.
3. **Add Grilled Vegetables:** Stir in grilled vegetables and soy sauce.
4. **Serve:** Divide among bowls, garnishing with green onions and chili flakes.

Ramen with Soft-Boiled Eggs

Ingredients

- 4 cups chicken broth
- 2 packs ramen noodles
- 4 eggs
- 2 green onions, sliced
- Soy sauce, to taste
- Nori sheets, for garnish

Instructions

1. **Cook Eggs:** Bring a pot of water to a boil, gently add eggs, and boil for 6-7 minutes. Transfer to ice water, then peel.
2. **Prepare Broth:** In a pot, heat chicken broth over medium heat.
3. **Cook Noodles:** Add ramen noodles and cook according to package instructions.
4. **Serve:** Divide noodles among bowls, add halved soft-boiled eggs, and season with soy sauce. Garnish with green onions and nori sheets.

Shrimp Tempura Ramen

Ingredients

- 4 cups chicken or vegetable broth
- 2 packs ramen noodles
- 8 shrimp tempura
- 1 cup spinach
- 2 green onions, sliced
- Soy sauce, to taste

Instructions

1. **Prepare Broth:** In a pot, heat chicken or vegetable broth over medium heat.
2. **Cook Noodles:** Add ramen noodles and cook according to package instructions.
3. **Add Spinach:** Stir in spinach until wilted.
4. **Serve:** Divide noodles among bowls, top with shrimp tempura, and season with soy sauce. Garnish with green onions.

Curry Udon Ramen

Ingredients

- 4 cups chicken broth
- 2 packs udon noodles
- 1 tbsp curry powder
- 1 cup mixed vegetables (carrots, peas, bell peppers)
- 2 green onions, sliced
- Soy sauce, to taste

Instructions

1. **Prepare Broth:** In a pot, heat chicken broth over medium heat and stir in curry powder.
2. **Cook Noodles:** Add udon noodles and cook according to package instructions.
3. **Add Vegetables:** Stir in mixed vegetables and cook until tender.
4. **Serve:** Divide among bowls, seasoning with soy sauce and garnishing with green onions.

Roasted Pork Ramen

Ingredients

- 4 cups chicken broth
- 2 packs ramen noodles
- 1 cup roasted pork, sliced
- 1 cup bok choy, chopped
- 2 green onions, sliced
- Soy sauce, to taste

Instructions

1. **Prepare Broth:** In a pot, heat chicken broth over medium heat.
2. **Cook Noodles:** Add ramen noodles and cook according to package instructions.
3. **Add Bok Choy:** Stir in bok choy until wilted.
4. **Serve:** Divide noodles among bowls, top with sliced roasted pork, and season with soy sauce. Garnish with green onions.

Tofu Ramen

Ingredients

- 4 cups vegetable broth
- 2 packs ramen noodles
- 1 block firm tofu, cubed
- 1 cup spinach
- 2 green onions, sliced
- Soy sauce, to taste

Instructions

1. **Cook Tofu:** In a skillet, sauté cubed tofu until golden brown.
2. **Prepare Broth:** In a pot, heat vegetable broth over medium heat.
3. **Cook Noodles:** Add ramen noodles and cook according to package instructions.
4. **Add Spinach:** Stir in spinach until wilted.
5. **Serve:** Divide noodles among bowls, top with tofu, and season with soy sauce. Garnish with green onions.

Spicy Kimchi Tofu Ramen

Ingredients

- 4 cups vegetable broth
- 2 packs ramen noodles
- 1 cup firm tofu, cubed
- 1 cup kimchi
- 2 tbsp gochujang (Korean chili paste)
- 2 green onions, sliced
- Sesame oil, for garnish

Instructions

1. **Sauté Tofu:** In a skillet, cook cubed tofu until golden brown.
2. **Prepare Broth:** In a pot, heat vegetable broth and stir in gochujang.
3. **Cook Noodles:** Add ramen noodles and cook according to package instructions.
4. **Add Kimchi:** Stir in kimchi and cooked tofu.
5. **Serve:** Divide noodles among bowls, garnishing with green onions and a drizzle of sesame oil.

Lobster Ramen

Ingredients

- 4 cups seafood broth
- 2 packs ramen noodles
- 1 lobster tail, cooked and chopped
- 1 cup shiitake mushrooms, sliced
- 1 cup baby spinach
- Soy sauce, to taste
- Green onions, sliced

Instructions

1. **Prepare Broth:** In a pot, heat seafood broth over medium heat.
2. **Cook Noodles:** Add ramen noodles and cook according to package instructions.
3. **Add Mushrooms and Spinach:** Stir in mushrooms and spinach until wilted.
4. **Serve:** Divide noodles among bowls, top with lobster, and season with soy sauce. Garnish with green onions.

Ramen with Dashi Broth

Ingredients

- 4 cups dashi broth
- 2 packs ramen noodles
- 1 cup sliced mushrooms
- 1 cup bok choy, chopped
- Soy sauce, to taste
- Nori sheets, for garnish

Instructions

1. **Prepare Broth:** In a pot, heat dashi broth over medium heat.
2. **Cook Noodles:** Add ramen noodles and cook according to package instructions.
3. **Add Mushrooms and Bok Choy:** Stir in mushrooms and bok choy until wilted.
4. **Serve:** Divide noodles among bowls, season with soy sauce, and garnish with nori sheets.

Lemon Chicken Ramen

Ingredients

- 4 cups chicken broth
- 2 packs ramen noodles
- 1 cup cooked chicken, shredded
- 1 lemon, juiced and zested
- 1 cup snap peas
- Green onions, sliced

Instructions

1. **Prepare Broth:** In a pot, heat chicken broth and stir in lemon juice and zest.
2. **Cook Noodles:** Add ramen noodles and cook according to package instructions.
3. **Add Chicken and Snap Peas:** Stir in shredded chicken and snap peas until heated through.
4. **Serve:** Divide noodles among bowls and garnish with green onions.

Duck Ramen

Ingredients

- 4 cups duck broth
- 2 packs ramen noodles
- 1 duck breast, cooked and sliced
- 1 cup bok choy, chopped
- Soy sauce, to taste
- Sesame seeds, for garnish

Instructions

1. **Prepare Broth:** In a pot, heat duck broth over medium heat.
2. **Cook Noodles:** Add ramen noodles and cook according to package instructions.
3. **Add Bok Choy:** Stir in bok choy until wilted.
4. **Serve:** Divide noodles among bowls, top with sliced duck, and season with soy sauce. Garnish with sesame seeds.

Creamy Spinach Ramen

Ingredients

- 4 cups vegetable broth
- 2 packs ramen noodles
- 1 cup cream or coconut milk
- 1 cup spinach
- 1/2 cup grated Parmesan cheese
- Garlic, minced

Instructions

1. **Prepare Broth:** In a pot, heat vegetable broth and stir in cream and garlic.
2. **Cook Noodles:** Add ramen noodles and cook according to package instructions.
3. **Add Spinach:** Stir in spinach until wilted.
4. **Serve:** Divide noodles among bowls, stirring in Parmesan cheese before serving.

Sweet Potato Ramen

Ingredients

- 4 cups vegetable broth
- 2 packs ramen noodles
- 1 sweet potato, peeled and diced
- 1 cup kale, chopped
- Soy sauce, to taste
- Green onions, sliced

Instructions

1. **Cook Sweet Potato:** In a pot, add sweet potato and vegetable broth. Bring to a boil and simmer until tender.
2. **Cook Noodles:** Add ramen noodles and cook according to package instructions.
3. **Add Kale:** Stir in kale until wilted.
4. **Serve:** Divide noodles among bowls, seasoning with soy sauce and garnishing with green onions.

Cilantro Lime Ramen

Ingredients

- 4 cups vegetable broth
- 2 packs ramen noodles
- 1 cup cooked chicken, shredded
- Juice of 2 limes
- 1/2 cup cilantro, chopped
- Jalapeño slices, for garnish

Instructions

1. **Prepare Broth:** In a pot, heat vegetable broth and stir in lime juice.
2. **Cook Noodles:** Add ramen noodles and cook according to package instructions.
3. **Add Chicken:** Stir in shredded chicken until heated through.
4. **Serve:** Divide noodles among bowls, garnishing with cilantro and jalapeño slices.

Beef Brisket Ramen

Ingredients

- 4 cups beef broth
- 2 packs ramen noodles
- 1 cup beef brisket, cooked and sliced
- 1 cup bok choy, chopped
- Soy sauce, to taste
- Green onions, sliced

Instructions

1. **Prepare Broth:** In a pot, heat beef broth over medium heat.
2. **Cook Noodles:** Add ramen noodles and cook according to package instructions.
3. **Add Bok Choy:** Stir in bok choy until wilted.
4. **Serve:** Divide noodles among bowls, top with sliced brisket, and season with soy sauce. Garnish with green onions.

Ramen with Braised Egg

Ingredients

- 4 cups chicken broth
- 2 packs ramen noodles
- 2 soft-boiled eggs, peeled
- 1 cup mushrooms, sliced
- Soy sauce, to taste
- Sesame seeds, for garnish

Instructions

1. **Prepare Broth:** In a pot, heat chicken broth over medium heat.
2. **Cook Noodles:** Add ramen noodles and cook according to package instructions.
3. **Add Mushrooms:** Stir in sliced mushrooms until tender.
4. **Serve:** Divide noodles among bowls, adding soft-boiled eggs on top. Season with soy sauce and garnish with sesame seeds.

Sichuan Spicy Ramen

Ingredients

- 4 cups chicken broth
- 2 packs ramen noodles
- 2 tbsp Sichuan peppercorns
- 1 cup ground pork
- 1 cup bok choy, chopped
- Chili oil, to taste
- Green onions, sliced

Instructions

1. **Prepare Broth:** In a pot, heat chicken broth with Sichuan peppercorns over medium heat.
2. **Cook Noodles:** Add ramen noodles and cook according to package instructions.
3. **Cook Pork:** In a skillet, cook ground pork until browned, then add to broth.
4. **Add Bok Choy:** Stir in bok choy until wilted.
5. **Serve:** Divide noodles among bowls, topping with chili oil and garnishing with green onions.

Buffalo Chicken Ramen

Ingredients

- 4 cups chicken broth
- 2 packs ramen noodles
- 1 cup cooked chicken, shredded
- 1/4 cup buffalo sauce
- 1 cup carrots, julienned
- Blue cheese crumbles, for garnish

Instructions

1. **Prepare Broth:** In a pot, heat chicken broth and stir in buffalo sauce.
2. **Cook Noodles:** Add ramen noodles and cook according to package instructions.
3. **Add Chicken and Carrots:** Stir in shredded chicken and julienned carrots until heated through.
4. **Serve:** Divide noodles among bowls, garnishing with blue cheese crumbles.

Ramen with Pickled Vegetables

Ingredients

- 4 cups vegetable broth
- 2 packs ramen noodles
- 1 cup pickled vegetables (carrots, radishes, cucumbers)
- 1 cup spinach
- Soy sauce, to taste
- Sesame seeds, for garnish

Instructions

1. **Prepare Broth:** In a pot, heat vegetable broth over medium heat.
2. **Cook Noodles:** Add ramen noodles and cook according to package instructions.
3. **Add Spinach:** Stir in spinach until wilted.
4. **Serve:** Divide noodles among bowls, adding pickled vegetables on top. Season with soy sauce and garnish with sesame seeds.

Black Garlic Ramen

Ingredients

- 4 cups chicken broth
- 2 packs ramen noodles
- 1/4 cup black garlic, minced
- 1 cup mushrooms, sliced
- 1 cup kale, chopped
- Soy sauce, to taste

Instructions

1. **Prepare Broth:** In a pot, heat chicken broth and stir in black garlic.
2. **Cook Noodles:** Add ramen noodles and cook according to package instructions.
3. **Add Mushrooms and Kale:** Stir in mushrooms and kale until wilted.
4. **Serve:** Divide noodles among bowls and season with soy sauce.

Garlic Butter Ramen

Ingredients

- 4 cups chicken broth
- 2 packs ramen noodles
- 4 tbsp garlic butter (or regular butter + minced garlic)
- 1 cup broccoli florets
- 1/4 cup grated Parmesan cheese
- Green onions, sliced

Instructions

1. **Prepare Broth:** In a pot, heat chicken broth over medium heat.
2. **Cook Noodles:** Add ramen noodles and cook according to package instructions.
3. **Add Broccoli:** Stir in broccoli florets until tender.
4. **Serve:** Divide noodles among bowls, mixing in garlic butter and topping with Parmesan cheese and green onions.

Smoked Salmon Ramen

Ingredients

- 4 cups fish broth
- 2 packs ramen noodles
- 1 cup smoked salmon, flaked
- 1 cup seaweed, shredded
- 1 cup edamame
- Lemon wedges, for garnish

Instructions

1. **Prepare Broth:** In a pot, heat fish broth over medium heat.
2. **Cook Noodles:** Add ramen noodles and cook according to package instructions.
3. **Add Edamame:** Stir in edamame until heated through.
4. **Serve:** Divide noodles among bowls, topping with smoked salmon and seaweed. Garnish with lemon wedges.

Ramen with Roasted Corn

Ingredients

- 4 cups vegetable broth
- 2 packs ramen noodles
- 1 cup corn kernels (fresh or frozen)
- 1/2 tsp smoked paprika
- 1 cup cherry tomatoes, halved
- 1 cup spinach
- Lime wedges, for serving

Instructions

1. **Prepare Broth:** In a pot, heat vegetable broth over medium heat.
2. **Roast Corn:** In a skillet, roast corn kernels with smoked paprika until slightly charred.
3. **Cook Noodles:** Add ramen noodles to the broth and cook according to package instructions.
4. **Add Vegetables:** Stir in cherry tomatoes and spinach until tomatoes soften and spinach wilts.
5. **Serve:** Divide noodles among bowls, topping with roasted corn. Serve with lime wedges.

Cilantro Coconut Ramen

Ingredients

- 4 cups coconut milk
- 2 cups vegetable broth
- 2 packs ramen noodles
- 1 cup green beans, trimmed
- 1 cup shredded carrots
- 1/2 cup fresh cilantro, chopped
- Lime wedges, for garnish

Instructions

1. **Prepare Broth:** In a pot, combine coconut milk and vegetable broth, heating over medium heat.
2. **Cook Noodles:** Add ramen noodles and cook according to package instructions.
3. **Add Vegetables:** Stir in green beans and shredded carrots, cooking until tender.
4. **Serve:** Divide noodles among bowls, garnishing with fresh cilantro and serving with lime wedges.

www.ingramcontent.com/pod-product-compliance
Lightning Source LLC
LaVergne TN
LVHW081339060526
838201LV00055B/2751